Praise for *Painful Gratitude*

Thumbelina has been a beacon of light to all who have had the opportunity to spend any time with her, whether young or old, whether five minutes or five years old. She lives life with a clear understanding of her everlasting destination. Through all of her adversities, she has never wavered. When reading *Painful Gratitude*, everyone will realize that the light she shares with everyone is the light of God, and that it shines upon her and through her continuously. I've had the honor of witnessing it for myself, as I have been a friend for over a decade and a sister in Christ.

—Angelique Williams

Pastor Thumbelina's love and passion for God is light that can be seen from a far distance. She inhabits a world of spiritual strength, authenticity and fearless grace. Her friendship and love have added to my life in so many ways, through laughter, tears, receiving the Holy Spirit and, most of all, gratitude to have her as my friend, sister and pastor.

—Theresa Lominy

As we go through life, we learn many lessons along the way. But it is a special blessing when God allows you to bear witness to the journey of His chosen. Now countless others will be able to learn the lessons that God has shown me through the life of Thumbelina Newsome. The one constant in her journey as a teenager, young wife and mom, divorcée, single parent, widow, entrepreneur and pastor has been her love for God and the manifestation of God's purpose. If you pay careful attention, as I have been blessed to do, you too will learn the lessons along the way.

—Jody L. Bell

Thumbelina is as unique as her name, and this book is a glimpse into her extraordinary life. She is a woman who is not afraid to live out loud. Her colorful personality will draw a crowd, and her light and love for Christ will brighten any room. She has the confidence to live with purpose, power and passion. To know her is to have a sister, a best friend and a watchman on the wall. I am extremely grateful for her friendship, and I'm sure after reading this book she will leave you wanting more! Go soar on wings like eagles and make God proud, Thumb! I love you.

—Rebecca Nazario

Pastor Thumbelina Newsome is a dynamic, powerful, Spirit-filled woman of God. Her commitment to excellence and enthusiasm for God and His living Word energizes everyone in her presence. The kindness, love and nonjudgmental attitude that she exudes are without measure and have helped so many people want to know more about God. We are proud to call her not only pastor but also one of our closest friends.

—Terrance & Melissa Thomas

Motivation at its best!
*A pastor for the future.
*One who relays what God wants us to know.
*It comes straight from a relationship with God.
*Inspired me to seek God with intensity.
*Spent hours talking on a daily basis and left me wanting to discuss more. Imagine yourself speaking to a person and never getting enough of it. One whose words fills you with the Spirit.

—Yris Pimentel

I will start by saying this: no one in the world will ever come close to the passion, love and obedience Thumbelina has for Christ!

My friend for thirty-plus years is the epitome of *strength* and *fortitude*. Throughout her life, she has constantly been handed lemons, with a side of more lemons! But in true Thumbelina fashion, she's always managed to make "loving lemonade" with the unwavering help of our Lord and Savior, Jesus Christ. She is now serving your supply to you, so that you too can experience the abundant love of our Savior.

I've always looked up to my best friend. But in this season, my eyes, mind and soul are locked in to witness and experience *God's love* that He has for one of His most prized disciples.

—Terisa Davis

To know Thumbelina for more than forty-plus years has been a true blessing to my life. Thumbelina's experiences have molded her into the fearless, confident and bold-hearted person she is today. I'm eager to see Thumbelina impact and transform the lives of others through her faith, testimony and love for God. Blessed is the individual who will come in contact with her; the world is now ready for Thumbelina.

~It's now time to fly, *Butterfly*.~

—Keiana R. Johnson

Thumbelina was a type of Thomas. She doubted everything and had to see it for herself. There are times as a parent we try to correct or fix something we see in our children, not realizing that God has placed it in them for His glory. Looking at her life, we can see Proverbs 18:16, that her gift from God is being used for His glory, and now she can tell the story. I believe she will draw more souls when they read this book. So keep the faith, stay in the race; the best is yet to come.

—Pastor Stanley & Faye Newsome
Resurrection Temple of Christ Church

PAINFUL GRATITUDE

A Memoir of Loss & Redemption

THUMBELINA NEWSOME

Copyright © 2022 by Thumbelina Newsome

All rights reserved. No part of this book may be used or reproduced by any means, graphic, electronic or mechanical, including photocopying, recording, taping or by any information storage retrieval system, without the written permission of the author, except in the case of brief quotations embodied in reviews.

Paperback ISBN 978-1-945169-98-4
eBook ISBN 978-1-945169-99-1

Published by
Mercy & Moxie
an imprint of
Orison Publishers, Inc.
PO Box 188, Grantham, PA 17027
www.OrisonPublishers.com

Scripture quotations marked (KJV) are taken from the King James Version of the Bible. Public domain.

Scripture quotations marked (NIV) are taken from The Holy Bible, New International Version® NIV® Copyright © 1973, 1978, 1984, 2011 by Biblica, Inc.TM Used by permission. All rights reserved worldwide.

I have compiled some of my life stories and experiences and have recorded the lessons learned from them.

*This is a book of inspiration and revelation.
My intention for this book is to encourage and inspire.*

Contents

Foreword xi
Note to My Younger Self xiii
1 God Had a Plan 1
2 All Good Things Must Come to an End 7
3 Obedience Will Take You to Your Purpose 13
4 Facing Reality 17
5 The End of a Chapter But Not the End of My Story 25
6 "I Surrender All" 33
7 Pain for Glory 35
8 Lessons I've Learned 41
Letter to God 49

Foreword

For as long as I can remember, I have been by my mother's side. I've watched the highs and the lows. I've seen the tears and the accomplishments. One thing has remained consistent throughout the years: God first.

My mother is someone with a lot of charisma and a magnetic aura. She is truly one of a kind and a gift from God to me and the world. I've had a front-row seat to witnessing pure will and drive mixed with faith, belief and love. Someone who has endured all that my mother has endured has all the right to be bitter. But she made the choice to always be better. Her constant elevation is no surprise to me because my whole life I have only witnessed just that: constant elevation.

My mother is a living treasure, and she truly personifies God's love. I just want to say thank you, Mom, for all your lessons; thank you for showing me that you are not your situation or your past; and, lastly, thank you for showing me firsthand that anything is possible when you put God first. God bless.

Your son,
Kase

Note to My Younger Self

Thumb, everything that happens in your life, happens the way you envision—but bigger.

You will be the epitome of every example God has called you to be.

You will love hard until you realize that you are loving the wrong people and things.

And with a ton of tests and trials, along with a few self-assessments, that strong love and passion you have for people will be transferred to God and God alone. The moment you transfer the love, you will begin to live on purpose. You will never love another human being or anything, for that matter, more than you love God.

You will love God so much that your passion and drive for Him will make you obey every assignment given, all the while yearning to hear the words, "Well done, thou good and faithful servant."

Keep being prideful, little girl, for life will humble you.

Keep crying, Thumb; you will figure it out. Keep trying to go back to college—you'll eventually get a degree. Once you get one, you will strive for more. Keep searching, Thumb; you will find what you were looking for. And once you find *Him*, meaning God, you will never be lost again. The mom you desired to be, you will become, and your children will call you blessed.

The struggles you are suffering with now are temporary. Just promise that you will never forget them. As you get older, your memory of your struggles will sustain you and keep you humbled.

They say the sky is the limit. But truth be told, there are no limits—only the ones you put on yourself. In time you will learn the value of your space. Never give anyone power in your space and never betray yourself in your space to make someone else comfortable. Only you can determine the energy in your space.

Before you are forty years old, you will have had some wins and some losses and will accept them all as lessons. Lastly, remember that your pain will eventually turn into gratitude and lead you right to your purpose!

1
God Had a Plan

Growing up, I lived with my parents and my three siblings in a four-bedroom home in Hillside, New Jersey. My stepsister lived with her mom but would stay with us sometimes during the summers. My parents worked hard, and we were an average middle class family. We took family vacations, played games and were faithful churchgoers. My father was also an assistant pastor of a church in Newark. It was a decent life. My father worked for University Hospital in Newark and retired as the supervisor of the morgue. My mother worked in the adult day care industry for thirty-plus years. After she retired in 2010, she founded Joy Cometh In The Morning, LLC, an adult day care center in Newark (which I later purchased and now own).

Life was decent until I became pregnant at seventeen years old in my senior year of high school. This was not a good look for my family. Here I was, the daughter of a preacher about to graduate high school, and I was four months pregnant.

My siblings and I grew up in a very strict household with a ton of restrictions, such as no pants, no nail color (clear only), no movies and no senior prom (just to name a few). My parents believed at that time that they were being obedient to God by following rules and doctrines that were actually man-made. But God blessed them for their obedience.

The shame and the embarrassment that I felt on behalf of my parents and my family were unbelievable. I knew they were going to get the backlash from the world, let alone from the church.

You can only imagine the scrutiny and snide remarks that we received during that time. I felt like the scum of the earth and believed I was the worst human being on the planet.

My parents were so disappointed and said, "There is no way around this; you will have this baby." They were so hurt! I just cried and cried, and for the next few days, I avoided them as much as possible.

One day I was in my bedroom bawling my eyes out, the pillow soaking wet, and my dad came in and sat on my bed. I cried and told him that I was so sorry for embarrassing my family and embarrassing him as a preacher. My dad's response was, "Listen, you are not the first and you definitely will not be the last to be pregnant out of wedlock. And who cares what the church thinks? Almost everyone in there has had a baby out of wedlock themselves, including me! We are the Newsomes, and we will get through this!"

Although my mom and dad were hurt, they still made sure that they supported me. They wanted to protect me from the world even through their embarrassment. When I look back, boy, am I grateful that I had parents who didn't throw me away because of my mistakes. They kind of remind me of someone else I know (wink, wink—God).

As time went on, I got a job as a customer service rep for a handbag distribution company. As I started to show, I became even more embarrassed. Now everyone knew that the little church girl was pregnant. So many snide remarks were made, by family, by friends and by the church. I think I cried the entire time in secret because I was so embarrassed and ashamed.

Just one month after my eighteenth birthday, I had a baby boy named Kase. I had so many mixed emotions. I was so young, bitter and angry, but I was determined to give him my best! After all, he didn't ask to be here. All along I had birthed a legend, and I didn't even know it.

Even through all of that, God had a plan!

At nineteen, I married Kase's father, but the marriage barely lasted a year. We divorced, and I was single again, but only for a short period of time.

By the time I was twenty-one, I had enough money to afford my own apartment. And yes, I was in another relationship with my live-in boyfriend and pregnant again with a little girl. (Don't judge me.) My frame of mind was different, though; I had a stronger mentality and knew that I was going to be okay this time around. This time, I knew I was carrying a brilliant and fearless queen. I could feel her energy inside me.

At twenty-one years old, I had my beautiful baby girl, Makayla, weighing six pounds, eleven ounces. I was engaged to her father, but the relationship didn't work out. A few months after her birth, I was back to being a single mother of now two children.

It was a struggle. I hated my situation. I had two children by two different men and wasn't with either of them. It was just a terrible space to be in (mentally and physically). But I remembered what my dad said: I wasn't the first and I wasn't going to be the last. I was determined to keep going! I did a lot of crying, but deep down inside my soul, I knew better days were coming.

By twenty-five years old, I found myself struggling to keep up. I was working full-time and could barely afford my apartment, car, child care and private school, let alone my monthly bills. I ended up getting my car repossessed. Embarrassed, I had to call my mom to ask her to take my kids to school. She said to me, "Do you really have that much pride that you couldn't ask me or Dad for help?" I had no response. She said, "I know you do not want to do this, but take your oldest son out of private school and move back home to save money. He is smart, and he will excel wherever he goes." So I did. I kept working and saved a ton of money.

I was ashamed that I had to move in with my parents with two children, but I never gave up on me.

It was a struggle, but again, God had a plan!

Not knowing who I was or who I was going to become, knowing that the journey ahead would be rough, something deep inside of me still knew that better days were coming.

Although I was living back home with my parents, I continued to work my way up in the company and started to make more money.

PAINFUL GRATITUDE

Determined that life had to be better than my mistakes, I was steadfast and eager to prove to myself and to my children that God was with us and that our story would end well because of Him.

The struggle was real. Did I mention that I cried all the time? In the car whenever I dropped the kids off and was alone, I cried. I had a ton of "shower cries." I cried in secret all the time, and God heard me.

Moving back home with my parents was actually a blessing. I was able to pay off all of my debts, pay rent to my parents, and save money. By the age of twenty-seven, I purchased my own, brand-new, three-bedroom townhome for me and my two children in Old Bridge, New Jersey. I remember, when I closed on my home, my dad was so proud that he wore a suit when he accompanied me to the closing for support. I couldn't wait to pick the kids up from camp to welcome them to their new home!

They were so happy, and life was beginning to look up.

I continued to work and did some part-time gigs on the side just to provide for my babies and to pay for this new home. I had many tough nights when I cried from exhaustion from working those jobs. I would work night jobs, get home in the morning to get my children dressed and ready for school, then get myself ready for my full-time job. I was so tired. At work, I would ask a friend to come into the restroom and wake me in twenty minutes, since I would go in there just so I could take a nap. Ugh. Talk about exhaustion!

I am so thankful for my sister, Shanna, and my mom, as they teamed up to help me. My mom watched my sister's only daughter (at the time) while my sister came to stay overnight to be with my two children while I worked. I am so grateful that I had that support from my family. Without them, I don't know if I would have made it.

Life was definitely looking better. I was dedicated and determined to serve God (although I still was not totally surrendered at this point).

Shortly after purchasing my new home, I bought a brand-new car and met an incredible guy named David. He worked at the BMW dealership in Edison. We dated and started a wonderful relationship. He was not like any guy I had ever dated. I was twenty-nine, and he was thirteen years older than me and very mature. He had no children and had never been married. He treated me and my children like we were the best thing since sliced bread. He was not intimidated by my independence. He actually relieved me of doing things by myself and just began to take care of us.

Within a few months of dating, he asked my son and my dad for permission to marry me. Of course, they both said yes! I'm sure they were like, "Somebody please take her off our hands."

He proposed, I said yes, and we got married. Life was so beautiful; better days had finally come. My heart was so filled with love. Married life with Dave was amazing. He took that girl who was a teen mom and grew her up. (I guess he knew that what was ahead of me required a real woman to handle.)

Even though I did not know what was ahead, I knew God had a plan for my journey.

2

All Good Things Must Come to an End

Here I was, married for the second time, and life with my husband was amazing! Dave was the most humble and meek guy you would have ever met. Kase was eleven years old, Makayla was six years old, and we all were so happy. Dave was such a wonderful stepdad to the children (not to mention a great cook). We never really argued. We had disagreements, but we talked through everything. Within our first year of marriage, at thirty years old, I gave birth to another beautiful baby boy named Logan. He was such a calm and peaceful baby. Dave was elated! Kase now had a little brother, whom he adored, and Makayla thought she was the mother of the baby. She was all over that little boy. Life had really turned around for the best.

Early in our marriage, Dave surprised me with tickets to see my favorite gospel artist, CeCe Winans. I was so hyped! He actually got me upgraded tickets with backstage passes, and I got to chat and meet with her. That place was filled with the presence of God, and it was that day, at that concert, that I totally surrendered to God and never looked back. What a day! When we left the concert, I remember driving home and saying to myself, "Life is amazing!" I had fallen back in love with the Lord; I had the husband of my dreams; and I had a beautiful family. What more could I ask for?

I was growing in Christ and being fulfilled at another stage of life. Dave spoiled the kids and me. He would make different meals for everybody every single day. We ate whatever we wanted, whenever we wanted it. Whatever any of us wanted, he made sure we had it.

I was special, though. I always had my meals served to me in bed. The kids would gripe about how spoiled I was, and Dave could care less. I was his baby, and nobody was going to stop him from taking care of me.

For our fifth wedding anniversary, he surprised me with a trip to London for nine days! It was an experience of a lifetime. We had so much fun watching the changing of the guards at Buckingham Palace, staying in a five-star hotel, and eating foods with an acquired taste. Again, life was awesome! I finally felt complete. I was serving God at my best, and I had such a supportive husband and a wonderful marriage. We studied the Word of God and prayed every night together. We were both growing in God. So many things happened in our marriage where God just showed up for us. Even our individual walks with God just grew!

We learned how to communicate effectively and had the best convos during pillow talk at night. We would talk about our goals and inspirations individually and collectively and made plans to conquer them. Life was great.

During our ninth year of marriage, we were in the process of buying a home in Monroe, New Jersey. We were so excited and tried to keep it hush-hush so the kids would be surprised. However, Dave developed a slight cough, and it was chronic. I said to him, "You've been coughing an awful lot lately." I cracked a joke and said, "I hope it's not Ebola." He laughed.

I told him to go to the ER one Sunday morning to get checked. He did. A few hours later, he called and said they told him that he had pneumonia and that they were keeping him overnight. I immediately packed some clothes and headed up to the hospital, which was two minutes from the house. After a few days, I'm like, "Why hasn't this cleared up?" He was there for about a week. We didn't understand why no one told us what was going on or why Dave was still there.

One evening while I was visiting Dave, the doctor came in. It was just the three of us in the room. I asked the doctor, "Why is Dave still here? Is the pneumonia clearing up? When will you discharge him?"

The doctor said, "Has no one spoken to you guys?"

We were like, "About what?"

He left the room, grabbed Dave's chart, came back and said, "You have stage four lung cancer, and it has metastasized to your bones."

With dumb looks on our faces, we were like, "Huh?"

Dave said, "Who, me?"

I asked, "What does metastasize mean?"

The doctor said it meant that the cancer had spread to his bones. "I'm sorry. You will need to see an oncologist. We will release you today," he said.

He left the room, and we both had this dumbfounded look on our faces. What the heck had just happened?

At the time I was working full-time and completing my last semester of college, taking four classes. I didn't know what to do. Dave looked at me and said, "How about you do some homework and not worry about what the doctor said?"

I didn't respond. We both were shocked, but I showed it openly.

Visiting hours were almost over, so I went home to be with the kids. I didn't tell anyone, because I had yet to take it all in. I took a shower and prayed. I said, "God, really? Cancer? I have been obedient, and I don't understand what You are doing, but I trust You." Then I went to sleep.

At five o'clock that morning, the Holy Spirit woke me up and said to me, "Tell My son David it's time to surrender."

I called Dave, and he was half asleep. "Hey, honey, you feel like chatting?" I asked.

He said, "Sure!"

I responded, "I need to tell you something."

"Go ahead."

I told him that the Holy Spirit woke me up and told me to tell him that it was time to surrender.

He replied, "Yeah, I know. I was supposed to do it earlier when your parents were here visiting and praying for me, and I didn't do it."

I said, "Well, I think we should hang up now and you should do it."

"Okay."

We hung up, and we never discussed what happened in that room that night between God and him.

The next day, he was released from the hospital. Dave decided that we should tell the kids and our parents about his recent diagnosis. So, we did. Everyone was shocked and devastated. The kids didn't want to hear it. We were all hurting for him. We couldn't believe this would happen to the G.O.A.T. (Greatest Of All Time).

We kept the faith, and we went to Memorial Sloan Kettering Cancer Center in New York City for treatment. Upon our arrival, we met his registered nurse, named Meghan Desimone. Immediately, we fell in love with her. The three of us clicked immediately like we had known each other forever. I would call her Meg, and she would respond with no hesitation! She was the absolute best. She gave him meds for his pain, and that day he started chemo. Dave said it made him feel tired, but we kept the faith.

For the next two and a half years, our wonderful lives were interrupted by going back and forth to New York for chemo and radiation treatments with our new buddy, Meg. She made our trips to chemo worthwhile. She felt like family to us!

There were times Dave didn't want me to see him like that, and, let's face it, I had to hold down the household and take care of the kids while Dave was in treatment. I needed help! Kase had his license and would drive Dave to treatments. Makayla only had a permit but would take Dave to treatments as well. He would be really nervous when Makayla took him. He used to tell me, "She was driving like a bat out of hell!" I would just crack up laughing. His best friend, Rich Russo, also helped us throughout our journey. The trips to New York City were very expensive. Between tolls and parking, the bills added up. Rich would take Dave to the city all the time and would not take a dime from us. What a blessing he was (and still is); they had such a special bond. He was a great cook too and made dinner for us so many times during Dave's cancer journey. The kids knew I was a terrible cook, so they would always ask, "Is Uncle Richie making food this week?" and I would laugh and say, "No, you will eat the nasty food Mommy made."

The struggle was real. I was still in school and wanted to quit, but Dave convinced me to stay in school. I did, and I graduated college. It was tough! It took a ton of prayer, faith and tears, but I got it done! Dave was so proud of me. On graduation day, my parents, husband and three children were there, ready to proudly cheer me on.

As I was walking in the processional, I could see my parents and the kids, but Dave wasn't with them. I remember, before sitting down in our seats, I pulled my phone out from under my graduation gown (which I wasn't supposed to do, but who cares) and texted him: "Where are you? I see the kids, but I can't see you." He texted back: "Just look up." And there he was on the balcony in a bright pink polo shirt with his thumbs up, standing and rooting for me!

By then the cancer was on his spine. It caused so much pain in his back that he couldn't sit. He was in excruciating pain, but he was determined to see his baby graduate. He said that he didn't want to block anybody's view by standing, so he went to the balcony to watch me.

My heart dropped. I began to get sad because he was in pain, but I also had gratitude in my heart because he was alive to watch me graduate.

After the graduation ceremony, he apologized that he couldn't take me out to dinner because he needed to go home and rest. My family took me out, but while we were at dinner I couldn't help but think, "God, is he going to die? Is this the end of my marriage? How will the kids take it? Will I have to go back to being a single mom?" It was so hard to enjoy dinner with these awful thoughts.

As tough as this new season was in our lives, we still kept the faith and gave praise to the Most High! We saw God work in ways you could never imagine. During this time, we tried to keep going and enjoy life while we traveled with caution. However, after a while, the chemo stopped working, and Dave's body began to decline.

I drew closer to God, and so did Dave. We trusted and accepted whatever God chose.

I knew that at some point, all good things must come to an end.

3

Obedience Will Take You to Your Purpose

Although Dave was sick, God was still working. As I drew closer and closer to God, I began to seek Him for answers. I found myself praying all day and night. Not just for Dave to live, but also to know why I was born. I wanted to know why I was sent to earth. Everything God told me to do, I did, no matter how crazy it seemed to anybody else. I loved Him and just wanted to know more about Him and where I had come from. One thing I have learned about God is that everything is a process and things are revealed in time. I heard someone say one time (I don't recall who) that God cannot be explained, that He must be revealed. As I sought God, He began to slowly reveal my purpose to me. One of my most memorable lessons was my first real lesson of obedience.

One sunny day I was on my way to the local drugstore by my home (I don't remember what I was going for) when an African-American woman got off a bus in front of the store. The only reason the moment caught my attention was because I had never before noticed a bus stop

PAINFUL GRATITUDE

there, even though I had lived in that town for a few years. I don't know why the lady who got off the bus caught my attention either, but she did. I pulled into the drugstore parking lot and parked. I got out of the car and went to the back of the store, where the pharmacy counter was, when the lady who got off the bus came over to me and tapped me on the shoulder.

"Excuse me," she said, "can you tell me where the cemetery is?"

Looking confused, I replied, "Sure! When you leave the store, make a right and go straight up Texas Road. It may be a few miles, but you can't miss it; it will be on your right-hand side."

She said, "Okay, thank you."

"Sure, anytime!" I responded.

At the time, I didn't think anything of our exchange. As I completed my transaction at the pharmacy register, I began to walk toward the front of the store to exit when I noticed that there were a ton of people in the store, any of whom this woman could have asked for directions to the cemetery. I thought it was weird that she would bypass all these people in the front of the store to come to the back and ask *me* for directions.

I got into my car, and the Holy Spirit promptly told me to pick her up. I said to myself, "Now this must be the devil talking to me, because I don't know this lady from a can of paint." Then I thought, "No, I am not going that way, so I am not going to pick her up." I heard the Holy Spirit say again, "Go pick her up." Reluctantly, I pulled up on the opposite side of the road as she was walking. I rolled my car window down and said, "Excuse me, miss?" She didn't hear me. Then I heard the Holy Spirit say to me again, louder, *"Pick her up!"*

I then shouted a little louder. "Excuse me, miss, would you like a ride to the cemetery?"

With no hesitation, she jumped right into my car. As she was putting her seatbelt on, she said, "The Holy Spirit told me you were coming to get me."

Somewhat startled, I said, "Yep, that's usually how He works!" We began to converse, and I asked her what her name was. She said her name was Dawn. I responded, "Nice to meet you, Dawn. I'm Thumbelina."

I looked at her and asked, "Who are you visiting today?"

Obedience Will Take You to Your Purpose

She replied, "My son. He was twenty-one years old and was shot and murdered at a bodega in New York."

I gently gave her my condolences and began to ask more questions.

She told me that he was her only son and that she had a younger daughter. She mentioned that she was from Staten Island, New York, didn't have a car, and was tired of depending on her family members and friends to bring her to New Jersey to visit him. So, she decided to take the bus. I asked her, "How do you do it? That has to be painful." She said that she was getting by because she was reading her Word and praying daily for strength, and that it was only by God's grace that she and her daughter were managing. I felt so bad for her and told her that I would keep her in my prayers.

As we were approaching the cemetery, I told her I had a good sense of direction at this cemetery because a close family friend was buried there a few months prior, and my children and I had gone to visit her a few times. I asked her, "What's his block number?"

"In block 19," she answered.

I said, "Perfect! My friend was buried in block 18, so I know exactly where it is."

As we pulled up to her son's block, I said, "Listen, it's a long walk back to the bus stop, and I literally live two minutes away. Once you are done, call me, and I will come get you and take you back to the bus stop."

With this surprised look on her face, she said, "Really? You would do that for me?"

"Absolutely!" I gave her my cell phone number, and she immediately called my phone. When it rang, I said, "Is your number 917…?"

She answered, "Yep. I will call you when I am ready to leave, and thank you so much."

"No problem," I said.

I left her and went home to await her call. Ten minutes passed. No call from her. Twenty minutes passed. Still no call. I figured she must have been there still grieving. Well, thirty minutes passed, and I decided to give her a call. When I called the phone number, the operator voice came on and said, "You have reached a nonworking number." With a puzzled and dumb look on my face, I said to myself, "She just called me from this number." I pressed the number again, and the recording came on again, saying that the number I had reached was a nonworking number. At this point, I was sitting there dumbfounded, like, how could this be? I wrote the number down on a piece of paper and dialed it again. I got the same response.

So, I decided to drive up to the cemetery. I went back to block 19 where I had dropped her off, and she was nowhere in sight. I rode around the cemetery and still did not see her. I drove up the street to see if maybe she had started walking back to the bus stop. Still no woman in sight. I put my car in park and just sat there in amazement. I wondered, "What in the world just happened?" I then realized that if I were to see her again, I would not even know what she looked like because I never saw her eyes. She had on shades the entire time.

Blown away, I went home and told my husband and the kids what happened, and they were stunned. They said, "It must have been an angel sent by God to test you." I called my parents, and they said the same thing. "It must have been an angel."

I could not believe that this just happened to me. There was clearly no evidence of this woman, no working phone number, and not a human in sight. I came to the conclusion that it must have been a test of obedience, and I passed it. I obeyed. Although reluctant, I still moved.

This test of obedience has been one of my greatest lessons in life thus far. It has made my ear keen to the Holy Spirit. Now, when God says move, there is no hesitation. I've learned obedience begets blessings.

This lesson was necessary, because God knew the journey ahead of me would require hearing His voice and obeying His command.

What I know for sure is that no matter how crazy it seems to yourself or anyone else, when you have a relationship with the Father, obey His voice, even if you don't understand His command, because obedience will take you to your purpose.

4
Facing Reality

As God was revealing Himself to me through the Word of God and personal lessons, Dave's cancer began to get worse. The treatments were no longer working, and he had begun losing weight drastically. He was in constant pain, miserable and constantly in and out of the hospital. I remember one day Dave said to me, "I know I'm going to die."

I answered back, "We all are; what's your gripe?"

"I just don't want that little boy to stop believing in God when I'm gone."

"So tell him about your God before you go." Then I asked him if he was afraid to die, and he said no. Then I stated, "Well, get excited."

"For what?" he responded.

I replied, "Because if you die, you get to see the face of God! That's what we've been living for, right?" He answered yes, so I said, "Don't look at this in a negative way, babe. God knows what He is doing, and He is in control."

Encouraging him was tough, but I had to stay strong. We pressed on. I continued to work every day and provide for the family.

PAINFUL GRATITUDE

One day I was at work at a world-famous, elite university in the Procurement Department (it was a side job to being an entrepreneur, just to make extra money to help out while Dave was not working). I went on a lunch break in the car by myself (which I always did) so I could pray and study the Bible. This particular day I was praying to God and I said, "I have been obedient to everything You have told me to do, whether I liked it or not. I have been a faithful servant. Can You please touch him and heal him? I know You can do it with just one touch. Please, God?"

Clear as day, I heard the voice of the Lord say, "No! My grace is sufficient enough for you, Thumbelina." In that moment, right in the car, I let out a loud cry! Then the voice of the Lord whispered in my right ear and said, "I have to take him home, okay?" Devastated, but trusting God, I said tearfully, "Okay. Your will be done, not ours. Just please help me and the kids with this, but most of all, give Dave peace! And Father, I trust You. Please be with us." I was a wreck.

I had to go back into work from lunch, so I stopped at the restroom, washed my face, got myself together and finished my workday. On the drive home, I knew I had to prepare myself as a wife and prepare my children and Dave for what God was about to do. I just didn't know when He was going to do it. I prayed all the way home, saying, "God, please help me and give us strength to endure what You are about to do. Please give my baby Dave the peace he needs until he gets home."

When I got home, I said to my two older children, "I don't think Dave is going to make it, guys. We have to prepare ourselves for the worst." I didn't want to scare them with what God had told me. I just wanted them to prepare in their hearts, as I didn't want them to be upset with God.

After I said that, they were so upset. They said, "Mom, you can't just stop believing in God! You have to keep praying and keep the faith." They both walked away from me. They didn't want to hear it, and I totally understood it.

Things were not going well at all with Dave, as he was back in the hospital in New York City at Memorial Sloan Kettering. The next day I called the doctor from work to see if she had any updates on his progress. When I called, the receptionist (who I got to know while on this

Facing Reality

journey) said, "Thumb, she wants you to come in to talk." My heart dropped. I just knew this was it and that she was going to give me a prognosis! Normally when I would call, the doctor would come to the phone and update me. So when she didn't come to the phone, I knew the news was going to be devastating.

I called and told my parents that the doctor wanted to see me, and they decided to drive me to the city for support. On the way there, the radio was on, my dad was driving, my mother was in the front passenger seat, and I was in the backseat looking out the window like a little kid. I knew the doctor was going to tell me what I had been dreading the most. As I was thinking about what the doctor was going to say, the tears began to flow nonstop. I knew this was it. I just didn't know how much longer we had with him. My heart was broken, and all I could think about was how sad and devastated Dave was going to be because he wanted to be here for his family. I was a silent wreck in that backseat. I could not stop crying silently, just thinking about my children. My seven-year-old was about to face the most traumatic moment of his life. I was beside myself.

Not knowing I was in the backseat crying, my mom asked a question (I don't remember what it was). When I didn't respond, she looked back and said, "Oh no, no, no. Don't cry, Thumb. You don't know what God has in store."

I said, "Mommy, it's time. This is the end, and I know it."

"We can't give up. The doctors don't have the final say. God does," she said.

I responded, "Mom, God told me He was going to take him home. He just never said when."

Immediately she became silent because she knew, since I was a little girl, I have always heard the voice of God.

My dad, with tear-filled eyes while driving, looked at me in the rearview mirror and declared, "T, everything is going to be all right. We just gotta trust God."

Crying, I said, "I know, Dad. I trust Him, but this still hurts."

We got up to the hospital room and Dave was there, just wasting away. My poor baby was trying to fight! The doctor came in and said hello to Dave and me, and then I introduced her to my parents. She sat on the edge of his bed and asked Dave for permission to speak about his prognosis in front of my parents, and he agreed that they could stay and listen.

I said, "Doctor, please don't B-S us. How much time do we have?"

She answered, "About three months. The cancer has outsmarted us and is aggressive, and Dave's body is too fragile for treatment."

Dave responded, "Just give me chemo. I want to fight."

"I can't give you anything else, because at this point it will hurt you," she replied. "I'll tell you what; if you can go home and eat, then I will order for you a small dose of chemo. Is that a deal? If not, you will have to go to hospice. You can go to a facility or stay at home."

He said, "I want to go home and fight. I will eat and take the chemo."

She answered, "Okay, then that's a plan."

Dave began to cry, and I gave the doctor some tissues to pass to Dave, since she was sitting on his bedside. I said, "Dave, tell the doctor what we do in times like these."

He responded tearfully, "In all we give thanks!"

She said, "You guys have given God thanks since this journey started. The two of you are too much. I love you guys and will do whatever you need, just keep me posted; and he will be discharged in the morning."

She hugged Dave and me, said her good-byes to all of us, and left the room. Right after she left, I asked my parents to leave the room as well so I could talk to Dave alone.

He said, "Don't tell my mom or the kids what she said."

I responded, "I understand not telling Logan because he's only seven, but Kase and Makayla can handle it. I have prepared them for this."

"Okay, just them, but not my mom, okay?" he repeated.

I'm not sure why he didn't want to tell her, but I just said, "Will do."

I kissed him and whispered, "We need to get you a haircut."

"For what?"

"Because the world is about to witness one of the greatest miracles ever performed," I responded.

"I hope so. I trust you, if you say that."

I knew that God was going to take him home (God had already told me He was). The miracle was that Dave was getting a two-for-one deal. I knew God was going to heal him and take him home at the same time.

Facing Reality

I could tell that Dave was devastated, though. He said to me, "Hold your hand out," and I did. He took off his wedding ring and put it in my hand. My eyes welled up, but I held in the tears. He stated, "Just take it. I lost so much weight, I can't fit it."

Jokingly, I responded, "Oh, you trying to get with some raggedy nurse up at this hospital? Oh, my brother, it ain't going down like that. I am going to get you a necklace to wear; you are not getting off that easy." We laughed, and he called me a nutcase.

But, deep down inside, I was torn because I knew what giving back that ring really meant. The marriage was over, and he had no more to give. My heart was secretly broken.

I told my parents to come back in the room to say good-bye to Dave for the night, and we left to go home. Let's just say it was a quiet car ride.

On the ride home, I called Kase to check in on the kids, since he was babysitting (he is the oldest, so he got that responsibility). He told me that everyone and everything was fine. Once I got home, I had a conversation with Kase (who was nineteen) and Makayla (who was sixteen) about what the doctor said, and they both were in disbelief and angry. Once again, they got up and walked out of the room. Again, I didn't say a word because I totally understood what they were feeling.

The next day, Dave was discharged and finally home. He was declining every single day. He was in constant pain, and things were getting worse. It seemed like nothing helped. He could barely walk and still was not able to eat. However, God heard my prayer about giving Dave peace. When I looked at him, my boy had that peace that surpasses all understanding, like Philippians 4:6 says. A week passed, and he still could not eat. He called me to the room, patted the bed with his hands, and said, "Come sit right here. I need to talk to you."

I said, "Okay. What's up?"

"Call the doctor and tell her that I am going to take the hospice."

I asked, "Are you sure? Have you come to terms with everything?"

He replied, "Yes, I'm tired."

"Okay, I will let her know," I said.

I left the room, went outside and sat in my car in the driveway, and screamed, "God, I can't take this!" Banging on the steering wheel and crying so hard, I just screamed over and over again, "God, I trust You! God, I trust You! God, I trust You!"

I stayed in that car until the tears subsided. Afterward, I followed Dave's instructions and called the doctor and told her that Dave decided to go into hospice. I also thanked her for all she had done. She had her team set up the hospice in our home.

Over the next couple of days, I began to notify close family members and friends that Dave was now in hospice and that we had up to three months before he would expire. I started making appointments for everyone to say their final good-byes. It was exhausting and devastating at the same time. But I remembered what God had told me. He was going to take His son home. I was going to be obedient and prepare for his homegoing service.

Dave and I had so many conversations during this time. I told him that he needed to talk to the kids because they were questioning what was going to happen. One day we called a meeting in our room. He whispered, before they all came into our room, and asked, "What should I say to them?"

I said, "Just answer truthfully to whatever they ask you."

Everyone came into the room (my dad and a friend from Georgia were visiting, so they joined us as well) and sat around the bed in chairs. I sat next to Dave on the bed, where he was sort of propped up. I began the conversation by saying, "Cancer does not rule this house; we rule it! We will communicate about everything from this time forward. Any questions you guys have for me or Daddy, we will answer them honestly. There is no need for just one of us to feel the pain. We can all help carry this load, and it will be easier if we are open about it."

Makayla said to Dave, "Are you scared to die?"

He replied, "No, because I don't feel like I'm going to die."

Then Logan asked, "Daddy, are you going to D?"

"What's D, buddy?" (Dave wanted to see if he knew what he was talking about.)

Logan answered, "Die."

Dave said, "I may, buddy. I don't know."

Logan walked over to me, hugged me, laid his head on my chest, and said, "I hate cancer. It sucks."

I responded, "I know, Logi."

Dave said, "Whatever you guys do, listen to your mom. This family has been blessed because of her. Whatever she asks you to do, just do it."

Everyone agreed and said okay. It was such a terrible moment in time, but it helped all of us. We all encouraged Dave and told him that we were there and that we had his back. He was very grateful.

When everyone left the room, I told Dave, "You did great, honey! I'm so proud of you!"

"Thank you," he said. "But it was only great because you were here."

I leaned over and gave him a kiss, then laid my head on his chest and began to cry! I sobbed, "I don't want this to end. I love you so much! What am I gonna do without you?"

He was crying as well. He said, "You're gonna keep going. In the beginning it will be tough, but over time the pain will stop."

"Are you worried about the kids?" I continued.

"No."

"No? Then what are you worried about?" He pointed to me. I said, "Me? Really?"

He then said, "The truth is, I never wanted to be married. When I turned forty, I didn't have any kids, and I came to terms with it. Two years later, I met you." Dave was crying as he continued, "You and the kids are the best things that ever happened to me, and now I have to leave this good stuff behind."

I had a yellow hand towel in my hand and shared the other end of it with him. We used the ends of the towel to wipe our faces as the tears just kept pouring. I said, "Can you do me a favor when you get there? Can you ask God to allow you to visit us in our dreams?"

He nodded. "If I remember, I will ask."

I sighed. "Okay. Is there anything you want me to do?"

He replied, "Keep shining and don't let nobody stop you."

Because I am such a clown, I started to sing the lyrics from Rihanna's 2012 song "Diamond" real loud: "Shine bright like a diamond!"

Dave said with a smile, "Go sit your tail down. You're a fool." We laughed it off and afterward just sat in silence, taking in the moment.

Now that we had gotten our pain and fears out of our systems, we were equipped with the tools and the boldness to talk about cancer

PAINFUL GRATITUDE

and all of our actual feelings. The conversations between Dave and me and with our family gave us permission to communicate our pain and fears. Boy, was that a release! At that moment, the entire family made peace with whatever God was going to do. We had finally faced reality.

5
The End of a Chapter But Not the End of My Story

While Dave was in hospice at home, we had a nurse in our bedroom twenty-four hours a day to care for him. Talk about annoying. I felt like I was being watched by the feds 24/7. But I didn't care if those nurses heard me crying out to the Lord. I anointed and prayed over Dave every single day and continued reading the Bible to him like I normally did. From time to time, I would see Dave's tongue move as he worshiped with me, and his soft claps turned into taps of worship as he got weaker. I would even blast Maranda Curtis singing "You Are My Strength" (written by William Murphy) and worship God all the time in that room. When family and visitors would come by, they worshiped with us too.

One day I asked Dave's best friend, Richie, to come over and sit with Dave for a few hours while I took a break. Even though a nurse was always there, I thought Dave would love to have Richie by his side. Richie didn't know this, but I met up with my sister-in-law Kelly and we went to the funeral home to make funeral arrangements for Dave.

PAINFUL GRATITUDE

Afterward, I went to the Lord & Taylor store by myself and looked for a suit for him to wear. I found this really nice, soft-pink Ralph Lauren suit. The store associate walked over to me and said, "Hi, that suit is actually on sale."

I responded, "Great! I will take it."

She asked, "Who is the suit for, and what is the occasion?"

I simply said, "It's for my husband, for his funeral." She gave me a look and broke down crying. I said, "No, no, no, we don't cry; we give thanks. My husband is dying from cancer and is in hospice, and he will pass away any day now. But just know that God has been good to us. Our family is well prepared, and so is he. In all, we give thanks."

"Wow," she said, "you're an amazing human being. Can I hug you?"

I replied, "Of course!" I purchased the suit, gave her another hug as she gave me her blessing, and I went back home.

A few days went by. It had been a few weeks since Dave had been at home in hospice. He was sedated. He had not spoken in about three weeks. He had a feeding tube and was resting in his hospice bed while I was sitting on my regular bed in our room. On this particular day, the head nurse was there visiting, along with the regular nurse who normally attended to him. The head nurse came over to me and whispered, "Thumbelina, we need to talk with you." So we left the bedroom and went into the hallway. She closed the bedroom door.

I asked, "What's the matter?"

She replied, "We need you to stop feeding him. At this point, you are prolonging his life."

I was like, "What? I can't do that! Are you asking me to stop feeding my husband so he can die?" I began to cry. "I can't do that, ma'am. I feel like I would kill my husband."

She said, "Listen, you are not killing your husband. He is in excruciating pain, and the nutrients from the food are the only things keeping him alive at this point. He is just suffering in agonizing pain."

"Can we just give him one can of the supplement drink a day instead of the three cans we give him now through his feeding tube?" I responded.

She replied, "If that makes you feel better. Just know that he is suffering."

The End of a Chapter But Not the End of My Story

I said, "Okay, let me think about it."

At this point, I was a mess. I went into the bathroom and just cried my eyes out! I knew Dave was suffering, and I didn't want to be selfish. I went back to the nurse and told her, "Okay, you guys can take it from here. I can't be selfish. Do what you gotta do."

Then came one day in the summertime. It was the beginning of August 2017. Dave was at home, not talking, just lying there, in hospice. We had twenty-four-hour care from the nurses. Logan was in camp, Makayla and Kase were working summer jobs, and I was in and out of work to be with Dave. I told the nurse I had to leave and go run some errands and then I would be back.

When I got back home, I came upstairs where the nurse greeted me with a strange look. Her eyes were wide open, like she had seen a ghost. I looked at her and said, "Oh no, did he pass away?"

She answered, "No, but he is talking."

"What? Talking? He hasn't spoken in weeks!" I went into the room and said, "Hey, Poopie, are you okay?"

Dave replied, "I'm ready to go home."

"You are home, honey. Do you mean go home to be with the Lord?"

He reached his arm up from under the covers and said, "Yes, I just want to rest."

I said, "When those angels come for you, you better fly high and don't look back."

"I won't."

"Heaven has no time; we will be right behind you. Let me tell you what it's gonna be like when you get to heaven," I continued. "The moment you arrive, all the angels are going to be silent. Then God Himself is going to give you the incorruptible crown of glory and put it on your head, and He'll say, 'Well done, thou good and faithful servant!' Then all the angels are going to scream, 'Woo hoooo! Yayy! You made it!'"

Dave opened one of his eyes, looked at me, and said, "I look forward to it!" Then he said, "Thank you for everything. I love you."

I answered, "No, thank you for everything. I love you more. Fly high!" I then told him, "I don't think Logan would be able to take you passing in the house. To be honest, it may be too much for all of us."

He said, "Do what you gotta do; send me to a facility."

"Okay," I replied, and that was the last time we spoke.

We had him transferred to a facility close by our home, where they made him comfortable. On August 9, 2017, and I don't know why I did this, I let Logan stay home from camp. The two of us stayed with Dave at the facility the entire day. Dave was sedated and just laid there.

Logan (who was seven) brought his crayons, coloring pencils, video games and Pokémon cards with him to play with while we sat. He and I were so greedy, we would go up and down to the cafeteria all day. Logan would make pictures and lay them on Dave's chest, saying, "Daddy, that's for you." That was the day he found the Pokémon card named "The Turtonator." Our last name was Turton, and, boy, was he excited to tell Dave. Although Dave could hear him, he wasn't able to talk back. Logan told his daddy about the card he had just found and placed the card on Dave's chest. I felt that this kid knew his time with Daddy was about to be over.

The next day, August 10, 2017, I went up to the facility to sit with Dave. My son Kase got Logan ready and dropped him off at camp. Afterward, he picked up Makayla from home and came, since they were both off that day and decided to sit with me at the facility. I don't believe this was a coincidence that they were both off that day.

Kase said, "Ma, today when I was getting Logan ready for camp, he was crying all morning."

I was like, "Really? Why?"

"I don't know," he said. "I just calmed him down and took him to Dunkin' Donuts to make him happy before I dropped him off."

Silently, we looked at each other. We all found Logan's behavior very strange.

While we were in the room chatting, Richie came in to visit. We greeted him and sat around for a few hours, just hanging out in the room. I left the room to chat outside with the nurse, and Makayla came rushing out to say, "Excuse me, Mom, something is wrong with Dave!" The nurse immediately ran in and took a look at him. He was shaking, and I'm asking, "What is going on?"

The nurse said, "It's time."

"Time for what?" I asked.

She replied, "He is going into cardiac arrest; he is about to go."

The End of a Chapter But Not the End of My Story

As Dave's breathing became more and more labored, I told Richie and the kids to cheer him on. We were all screaming, "Go, Dave! Go! Go! Go, you've got it. Don't be afraid! Fly high!" Dave was inhaling and exhaling extremely hard. Every breath was a struggle. He was gasping for air. Richie was saying, "Go, buddy! You've got it!" And then it happened: he took his last breath! The room went silent, and then his body went limp. I said, "That's it, guys. He's gone." I grabbed Dave's hand while my tears were falling and said, "Thank You, God. Thank You, God. Thank You, God, for the gift of Dave. Well done, honey, you did it!"

It was 11:55 a.m., and the nurse told us we had to wait five minutes before she could declare him dead. We waited in silence until she said, "August 10th, 2017. David A. Turton expired at 12 p.m."

I looked over at Kase, and he had his shirt over his face, crying with his veins popping out on his forehead. He was so distraught! Sobbing uncontrollably. So was Richie. I went to hug Kase, and I looked over to see Makayla straightening Dave's body out, talking to him, saying, "You did a great job!" She was fixing his gown and getting his body prepared for the funeral home. She said she didn't want rigor mortis to set in. So, she let the bed down and laid him flat. She didn't shed a tear. That girl was so strong. While we were calming down and taking in Dave's death, I called my parents to tell them the news. Then I called his parents. They all came rushing to the facility to say their final good-byes.

Richie couldn't take it; he said, "I have to go, dear." We hugged him and thanked him. I asked him to reach out to the church for me to let them know that Dave had passed. He said that he would and left.

The kids and I stayed a little longer as the staff gave us as much time as we needed to say our good-byes.

When I told the kids that I was ready to leave, they packed my bag and whatever belongings Dave had there. We were about to walk out the door when my heart just broke! I screamed, "Wait! I'm not ready to leave yet! I can't do this!" Kase and Makayla grabbed my arms, saying, "Mom, we don't have to leave. Let's stay here until you are ready." I needed to kiss Dave one last time while he was still warm. We stayed for about a half hour longer, and finally, I was ready to leave.

Kase and Makayla walked me to the car. I was in shock. Kase opened the car door and Makayla put my seatbelt on, and we drove home. As we were on the way home, I burst out again in tears. I screamed again, "Oh my God, we have to tell Logan!" I was done! Once again, Kase and Makayla said, "Mom, don't worry. We will take you later to pick him up from camp. Don't worry; we've got your back." We were all devastated. Although God told me He was going to take Dave home, and I prepared as much as I could, it still felt unreal.

When we got home, I saw my mom pulling up at the house. When I got out of the car, my legs felt like spaghetti. My mom didn't say a word. She was just by my side. We went in, I sat on the couch, my mom sat next to me, and I laid my head in her lap. I let out this loud scream and began to sob uncontrollably. I could not believe that the man who finally came and changed my life was gone. And I knew that I still had not told Logan. It was just awful.

Eventually the time came for us to go pick up Logan from camp. Kase drove Makayla and me, and, once we got there, Kase went inside to get him. They came out, and Logan got in the car with so much excitement. "Mommy," he exclaimed, "I won at the gaga pit today!" We were all like, "Oh wow, that is awesome, Log!" He said, "It was the best day ever!" I felt so bad inside because this kid had no idea what was coming.

He asked, "Why is everybody here to pick me up?"

"Because Mommy has to tell you something," I answered.

Kase pulled the car over and parked. Logan said, "Daddy died today, didn't he?"

"Yes, son, he did."

"Can I go see him?"

"Not right now," I replied. "You will see him for his funeral because first they have to clean him up. But Makayla took a picture of him after he died, if you want to see it."

He said, "Yes, I want to see him." I showed him the picture on my phone, and he responded, "He looks the same; he looks like he is sleeping."

"Yep, Daddy isn't in pain anymore. He is in heaven with God now."

The rest of the car ride home was silent.

For the next couple of days, I put everything in place for the funeral service. I called it a homegoing celebration because I knew Dave went home to be with God. When Dave was first diagnosed, he gave me instructions on what he wanted and how he wanted things to be done if he were to pass away. He asked to be cremated after the service. I followed his instructions.

I also had to make sure there was no obituary. Dave and I had the same funeral request: no obituary; just pictures that said, "May the Works I've Done Speak for Me." We believe it doesn't matter what college we went to or what we did for a living. If our lives didn't point to Christ, then we were useless. I made sure that his requests were carried out.

On the morning of the day of the service, the kids and I got up, got dressed and waited for the funeral home's black Escalade truck to pick us up. My friend Yris from Georgia had flown in the day before to be with me and my children. She rode with us on our way to the service. The truck had a third row. Yris, Makayla and Logan sat in the last row, Kase and I were in the second row, and the driver was up front.

As we were driving, I put my head down and began to pray. "God, please don't let this day be about us or the man who died. You deserve all the glory. For it is all about You and not about us."

Kase reached over, thinking that I was crying, and said, "Mom, are you okay?"

"Yes, son. I'm just praying that God is glorified today, not us!"

"Okay," he said.

What a beautiful homegoing celebration it was! Over four hundred people were there. Our good friend Meg (his registered nurse from Sloan Kettering) shared words at the service, and she was awesome! My dad did the eulogy while my mom did what she does best. She sat next to us, on the front pew, silent and supportive. We also sang and rejoiced like you wouldn't believe, and God showed up! God answered my prayers and held the tears back from my children and myself.

We were at peace because we knew that Dave's painful fight was finally over and that God got the victory! What most people don't know is, we had a funeral way before they did. We cried our entire journey, and not only did God free Dave, but He also freed us from the agony of watching his awful journey.

That night after the funeral, I was home in my bedroom alone. I turned off my phone because I didn't want to be bothered with anyone and laid on the bed taking everything in that happened. I had so many thoughts running through my mind. I had so many questions for God. I was thinking, "Wow! Did my husband just die, and we had a funeral today? God, what are You doing? How are my kids going to be after this? What will this do to Logan? Do we all have to go to therapy now?" It hit me like a ton of bricks. As I began to cry again, I said to myself, "You are back to being a single mom of three now, and you're a widow." All the pain from my past showed up. I started to think, "Did I just go through all that for no reason?"

Then that same deep feeling that I always had when things didn't go right, returned to me and said, "No, Thumb, you didn't go through that for nothing." In that moment, I had to encourage myself and say, "Thumb, the same God who was with you before will get you through this." My own encouragement gave me the peace that surpasses all understanding. That peace reminded me that this is just the end of a chapter, not the end of my story.

6

"I Surrender All"

Life after Dave's passing was challenging. I had so many moments of grief without relief. It was hard! I remember saying to myself, "I just wish somebody who knows me well would tell me I will be okay." Even though I knew it, I felt like I needed to hear that. For some reason or another, when someone who didn't know me well told me that, it was hard to take. Why? Because I knew they didn't know me well. I wished somebody would say, "You're allowed to grieve," or, "Give yourself permission to grieve." I wished somebody would have told me what I told my children: "It's okay to cry. Cry until your tears are dry." Oh, how I wished somebody would have just said, "Grieve as long as you need to. Girl, you just took a huge loss."

The truth is nobody told me that because they didn't see me in the moment. They saw me in the future, so they spoke to me as if I were already there. People who knew me well had a hard time consoling me because they knew me for my strength and tenacity. It was like a catch-22. I wanted to hear it, but I wanted to pick who said it. Well, you can't have your cake and eat it too, Thumbelina.

PAINFUL GRATITUDE

The grief that I felt was not just the loss of my husband, my lover, my right arm, the father of my children, my partner and the love of my life. This bereavement period was also for the loss of my friends, money, my family, my children or anything that I ever loved more than anything in the world. I felt like I'd lost everything, including myself. However, I think that's the space God wanted me to be in.

I have discovered that there is only one space in my heart, and that's for God and God alone. I now have learned the art of surrendering, which is a daily act. Because of the love I have for my Father God, I have chosen to surrender all. Nothing or no one will ever be in the center of my heart. I love Him more than anything in the world! Since Dave died, my only desire has been to please God. I am rubble and have nothing. The only thing I have to give Him is myself. And because of all the great things that God has done, especially because of who He is, I owe Him me. That is my only sacrifice to offer. So now I have a new life hierarchy: God first, then Thumbelina. Everyone else (including my children and family) gets my overflow. Because apart from Him, I can do nothing! I must stay connected to the Father.

The only thing that is sure and true is that God loves me. In my soul, I felt like God already grieved for me before He told me He had to take Dave home. In my flesh, I feel like it was a tough gig for God to tell the child He loves that He had to take another one of His children home. But I can hear God saying, "If only she could just trust Me after this. There is something great in store. If only she could see her life through My lens."

You see, my pain won't stop my progress. I understand the call that is on my life. And I know that I must do the work that God created me to do. It's like wedding vows. I have to stay with God for better or for worse, in sickness and in health, for richer or poorer, and even after death. I must be committed to the process and not the pain. I have seen God and His favor all over me and my children. I am truly blessed and loved by the Father, and I know it. And for that, just like the old hymn, "I surrender all."

7
Pain for Glory

As painful as losing Dave was, I found me. I had to reinvent myself as an entrepreneur, a woman and a mom. I wasn't sure what God had planned next for my life, but just like in everything else, I trusted Him.

After Dave's death, all three of my children had their own personal journeys of grief. It showed up differently for all of us. We had to learn how to live without Dave. However, I only gave my children God, for He was all I had to give. I made sure everyone had access to therapy, and my two eldest children had a choice if they wanted to go or not. Logan had no choice. He and I went on the regular. It really helped by giving us the tools we needed to grieve. With therapy and prayer, we got through it.

My relationship with God grew so much from this experience. I became relentless in finding my purpose and doing God's will. I went into straight pursuit of purpose, and, after diligently searching, I found it! The truth is, I actually pursued God first and then found me, which led me to my purpose. The key was connecting to the Creator and asking questions like, "Who are You?" or, "Why did You create this world the way You did?" and, "Why was I sent to earth?"

One day in my pursuit of finding God, I heard the Holy Spirit say to me, "Everything you were taught has brought you here to Me in this moment. I need you to unlearn what you were taught, and I will teach you who I am." I felt like He was saying, "You were looking for Me, and you found Me. Now let Me show you who I am. Let Me show you My power, and, most of all, let Me show you who you are and the power that lies within you." I was so hungry for Him. I had such a thirst and a longing to know more. I prayed all the time and spent every chance I could with Him. I was at my highest peak spiritually. I would read the Word of God every single day—sometimes two or three times a day. It was like water to my thirsty soul. I had begun to have clarity regarding things in life. The pages in my Bible were soaking wet every time I read it. I was in awe of how God allowed me to comprehend His Word so clearly. But I knew that I was only receiving such clarity because I was putting in the work.

I found myself wanting more, more, more. Just hungry and thirsty. But, of course, you know the enemy didn't like how much time I was spending with the Lord. I knew the deeper I grew in God, the more dangerous I became to the enemy.

I had to make a conscious decision. I decided that I was going to turn my ear off to man and only listen to the voice of God. I believed that if man had a message for me, then God would let me know. I believed that God would warn me when they were on the way with a message and for me to listen to it. God was pruning me, and He used my pain to get me to His glory.

As I continued on this path, the enemy started putting distractions in my way. My children had issues with their grief and needed more of me. My oldest son dropped out of college to pursue music when he had only eight classes left to graduate. He too was in pursuit of God and himself. My daughter graduated high school and was going to a college ten hours away. That was too far! I was so worried about her. It was too much! Logan was trying to live life without Daddy, and he was silently struggling and grieving all the time. I was struggling with my own grief. For an entire year, I slept with pillows lined up like a body next to me because I would grieve so hard at night. I was literally grieving and growing at the same time, just taking one day at time so I could heal.

I was overwhelmed in the flesh, and all I could do was stay connected to God. That was all I wanted to do. My connection to God was my only source of strength and relief at the time. Anything else would take time away from my pursuit of God and my purpose, and I wasn't having it.

I was so broken about my children's struggles. But I was only able to give them minimum pieces of me. I had nothing to give them. I needed to find me. I knew that you could only give from your overflow and not from an empty cup. I had nothing. I was struggling to give myself care, let alone give care to my children. I literally took a year off from parenting. I know you are thinking, "Why in the world would you do that when they needed you the most?" Well, I had no choice. If I didn't do it, they would have been at risk of losing another parent. Not of me physically dying, but of me totally losing myself.

I made sure there was food in the house and that they had the necessities. I still took Logan to counseling when needed, and I just survived. I had no big mommy hugs and kisses. I had no advice to share or give. I don't think I even cared about my day or theirs. I washed clothes and provided for them, but nothing extra that they were used to getting from me.

I went to work when I felt like it because I owned the company, but I did the bare minimum there too. I just wanted God and what He had purposed for me. At this point in my life, I had set myself up fairly well financially and was in a very good space, so money wasn't a problem. I was diligent. I needed to find God so I could find me.

I increased my travels worldwide and saw God everywhere and in everything. I met so many new people, and as I traveled the world, my perspective on God changed. I studied more. I prayed more, and I could hear Him even clearer. As time moved on, I found myself healing day by day.

A year and a half after Dave's death, I was beginning to get my joy back. My relationship with my children changed. I became the mother they needed and not the mother I thought I was supposed to be. I came back better.

When I was married to Dave, I would always go to bed so happy at night, and he would say, "Look at you, always Chuck E. Cheese-in."

PAINFUL GRATITUDE

Boy, do I miss those days. I remember one night as I was healing, I felt myself smiling as I was lying down in the bed, preparing to read a book, and all of a sudden I realized my joy of going to bed was coming back.

In that moment I realized I had power over grief. As God began to show me who I was, I started speaking and using the power of my tongue. As I was learning and growing, I began to teach my children who they were and about their internal power. I began to learn the art of manifestation. If I thought it and believed it, then it was mine (as long as it was in the will of God). I started to declare victory over grief. I believed there would be sunshine after the rain. I started to believe that I had power and that I was the master of my own fate. I spoke over my children and declared their victory over grief. I prayed for God to heighten His protection around my children and me because I knew, at that point, that I had tapped into something most people don't.

I learned how to become present. I continued to go to counseling so I could get tools for grieving properly. I applied the tools, and with prayer I began to see and feel change. I sought so hard after God until, one day, I had an epiphany. The light bulb in my brain had finally come on. I was excited! I found Him! He was in me all along. Every mistake I made, He was right behind me with a plan. In every heartache and every disappointment, He was there, living inside of me all along.

During this period of healing, God called me to pastor. To be honest, He had been calling me for a few years prior, and I ignored it because I didn't want the job. I just wanted Him. I had a hard time accepting this call because I was so worried about people and what they were going to say. I didn't feel like I was equipped for such a big task. I would tell God over and over, "You got the wrong chick." And He insisted that He chose me as a child for such a time as this. I had conversations about me pastoring with my children, some friends and my parents. I even went to Israel and spoke with a rabbi to ask his opinion about it. The consensus was for me to obey.

I still didn't move, though. One day, I could feel God urging me so strong to answer the call. I was shaken—so much so that I went running to my parents' house. I asked my parents to fast and ask God to confirm to them that my being a pastor what was He wanted from me. My dad agreed that he would fast, but my mom said, "I'm not fasting. I knew this is what you were supposed to do since you were born, and I was praying that I would be alive to see it."

As time went on, the urges from God got stronger and stronger until, finally, I surrendered to His will. A few weeks later, my dad heard from God, and he confirmed that this was what God was calling me to do. I had to think that if God had brought me through every test and trial in my life, how could I not obey His call?

I was scared out of my mind. However, the call was bigger than me. It was bigger than my thoughts. It was bigger than what people were going to think or say. It was even bigger than death. I knew that I owed God me.

I obeyed, and I was ordained on August 10, 2019. It was two years exactly from the day Dave died. That was the date God gave me, and, of course, I didn't understand why He chose that date. But if you know me, you know I'm trusting God no matter what. A few weeks later, God gave me the name "Transformed Generation," and the church was started on November 3, 2019, in Old Bridge, New Jersey. I stopped questioning and started obeying as my purpose was beginning to be fulfilled.

Not only was I doing what I was born to do, I also was now living on purpose. It was hard, but it felt right. Although I had found God and answered the call on my life, I was still in pursuit of self.

Being a leader is such a tough job! I was going through the highs and lows of the calling. Still, I was born for this! God told me to go back to college to study theology and of course I obeyed. I went back, and something happened to me. On January 10, 2022, while in my first online class, I had another epiphany, and the tears started flowing because I had just realized who I was. I felt like the struggle was over. I saw clearly how the enemy had tried to distract me from getting here prior to this moment. I passed every test that was given to me. I trusted God throughout my entire process and I had done the work. I realized that the fight I had in me made me a threat to the enemy and that no devil in hell could stop me. All of my trials and traumas were going to be used to help heal the world through ministry. And I got it!

PAINFUL GRATITUDE

No more listening to people or the enemy! I will trust God like I always did in life, and it is guaranteed He will show up for me. He has never failed me. It was my time, and the world was about to meet me. As the tears did not stop, I heard the Holy Spirit say to me, "Well done, daughter. Obedience has brought you here." I cried through the entire class.

I realized that God was in me and with me. As I stated earlier, I owe Him me. In March of 2022, I went to Morocco, North Africa. On the way there, I prayed and asked God to meet me there. I told Him that I wanted to see Him in the water and in the walls. I remember the day we arrived at the hotel. I was in my room, in the restroom, and I said, "I'm here, Lord. Where are You?" The Holy Spirit said to me, "Never ask Me to meet you anywhere. Take a picture or look in the mirror. I am in you always."

I was in awe of God and in awe of me because I had finally found what I had been desperately searching for: God and myself.

My entire life was set apart by God with experiences that would be used for His glory, not mine. With God, *nothing* was wasted! God's work will be done in me and through me. My pain had finally turned into gratitude, and God had finally received all the glory from it!

Jeremiah 1:5 (NIV): *"Before I formed you in the womb I knew you, before you were born I set you apart; I appointed you as a prophet to the nations."*

8

Lessons I've Learned

Know the Voice That Whispers
Have you noticed that, throughout your life, you have always had gut feelings or intuition about something or someone? Have you ever heard something deep down inside of you warning you about trouble? Or how about having an inkling, knowing something or someone isn't right?

The real question is, when you heard that whisper or got that inkling, did you listen to it?

What I know now, which I didn't know before, is the voice that whispers is who I call God. The Creator Himself. He always knows, speaks, guides and protects us. When we choose not to listen, suffering occurs, for we have violated our intuition.

The only way to trust the whisper or the voice that you hear is by obeying it. Once you obey it over and over, then you can trust it. But, before you can trust the voice, you must know who speaks. And you can only know who speaks by being in pursuit of God.

What I have learned is that God is self-actualization. The Bible says in Genesis, chapter 1, that we were made in His image. No other creation on earth was made in God's image but us. What an honor! If we truly understand this concept, then we understand how unique we are. And all that He is, we are, in smaller form.

Oftentimes I hear people say to me, "You make God seem like a real person." My response is, "Of course He is. He is more real to me than you are." I can only say this because of the time I spend with Him. For me, it's the daily encounter with Him that makes Him so real.

Over the course of your life, you will find that the world is noisy and oftentimes we can't hear Him. We are surrounded by distractions and therefore can't hear, or we will hear him and choose to ignore the voice.

My advice is to isolate yourself from time to time, in order to hear the voice of God. Once you practice hearing Him, the whisper will become louder than the noise around you. It will be so loud that you can be in the world's parade and when He calls you, you will march right out of it because your ears have become keen to the voice. No other noise can stop you. Spending time with Him is key.

Last year, 2021, I was so burdened with the daily dealings of being a pastor. I felt like the choice I made to not listen to man had offended a lot of people. I was a new pastor, and people felt that I should listen to them to help guide me on my journey. Yes, with my journey. Keep in mind that they never answered their own calling and were struggling with clarity from God for themselves, but they wanted me to listen to them. Whatever!

I was highly annoyed, and it was a very painful time for me. So, one day, I felt like if I didn't go away and seek God, I was going to have a nervous breakdown. The weight of the people was so heavy. I had to take a few days off from life. I didn't tell anyone but my children where I was going. I made arrangements for my children, my company and my church while I went away for a few days to an undisclosed location. There, I cut off communication with everyone (except my children). I got on my knees and cried out to the Lord. I told Him how heavy this calling was and how I must be doing something wrong. I told Him what I heard people saying and how they felt I was not listening to them. Sobbing, I told Him all the things that I am not.

God's response was, "You have told Me everything that you are not. Now let Me tell you everything that you are. You are chosen! You are unique because I created you that way. Your disobedience to man is in obedience to Me. Continue to do everything you have been doing. I will continue to guide you and protect you."

While I was in tears, God told me to go sit in a chair and hold out my hands. I did. It felt like my hands were on fire, and they had this tingling sensation. He said to me, "That is the power I give unto you."

Crying uncontrollably, I just started screaming, "Thank You, Father! Thank You, Father!" My heart was filled with such gratitude because, once again, I sought the Lord, and He heard me and showed up.

Psalm 34:4 (KJV): *"I sought the Lord, and he heard me, and delivered me from all my fears."*

God is the voice that whispers. Are you listening?

Know Your Value
Looking back at my life, I realized that I did not know my value or my worth. It wasn't until 2022 that I realized how valuable I was.

I didn't know my value because I didn't know who I was in Christ. One of the lessons I've learned in finding myself is this: people know who you are before you do.

Have you ever seen a kid and thought, "Oh, she is a tough cookie," or, "He will be a great entertainer one day"? Or you can even tell when a kid will be a troublemaker. We have all seen children and had those thoughts. Like I said, people know who you are before you do.

The question is, how did you treat me when you knew who I was?

After I found myself and realized how valuable I was, it hit me like a Mack truck as I went back into my thoughts of how many people knew who I was and devalued me!

In 1997 I went to Lincoln Tech for my certification in business, and I met a woman named Tracy Britten. Our birthdays were a week apart in November, and she was about ten years older than me. Our connection was instant; we just developed a sisterhood.

After we graduated trade school, we remained really good friends. We weren't the type of friends who spoke every day, but when we connected, it was always fun and laughter as we would catch up on each other's lives.

I remember in 1999 when I was almost twenty years old after my first marriage. I was looking for my first apartment, but I didn't have any real credit and didn't want to ask my parents for help.

Tracy knew I was a single mom of one child at the time and that I needed my own place. I found this beautiful apartment in Elizabeth, New Jersey. It had one bedroom with hardwood floors and high ceilings. It was a beautiful apartment. Although I could afford the rent, my credit wasn't good enough. I remember telling her that I applied for this apartment but that I needed a cosigner. With no hesitation, she said, "I'll cosign for you."

I'm like, "I didn't tell you this for you to cosign!"

She said, "I will do it."

"Really?" I asked. "You would do that for me?"

"Yep! No problem. I trust you!"

I promised her that if she did that for me, I would make her proud and would never screw up her credit. I also promised that she would never regret it.

She cosigned for me, and the landlord approved me for the apartment.

The landlord said that if I paid my rent on time for a year, he would take Tracy's name off as the cosigner, and I would be able to build my own credit.

I worked my butt off and I paid the rent on time for a year. Her name was taken off of the lease.

During that time, I was in another relationship and had my second child. Makayla was about a year old, and I remember one day going through such a horrific heartbreak with her dad that I didn't want to live anymore. I was so heartbroken. I was a mess. I was at home, lying in bed in a daze for hours.

As embarrassing as this story is to tell, I'm still going to share it in hopes of it helping you.

I locked myself in my bedroom and left my four-year-old in charge of the one-year-old. (Don't judge me.) I was sobbing in pain, telling

God that it was too much! I couldn't handle two children by myself! I hated that I had become a statistic! I felt like I was about to lose everything! I was just in pain.

I was totally zoned out, so much so that I couldn't even hear my children knocking on the door or crying.

I was out of it, and I wanted to end it all. But I knew I couldn't because those kids needed me. They didn't ask to be here!

For some reason or another this particular day, my friend Tracy called. I had not spoken to her in a while, but I guess God gave her an inkling to give me a call.

I didn't have the phone in my room, so my four-year-old son, Kase, answered.

Tracy: "Hey, how are you? Where is your mom?"

Kase: "I'm good. She is locked in her room and won't come out, and we are hungry."

Tracy (knowing something was wrong): "Okay. Auntie Tracy is coming over. Here is the password. When I get there, I will tell you the password. Get your chair and unlock the top lock for me, but only when I give you the password, okay? And I will bring you guys McDonalds."

Kase: "Okay."

They hung up. She got there, and he followed all of her instructions. He waited for the passcode and then opened the door.

She came in, said hello to the kids, then busted my door open and saw that I was in a terrible state of mind. I was a zombie.

She gave the children food, gave them baths and put them to bed. After she took care of them, she came to my room to help me out.

It wasn't until after everything was over that Tracy told me her side of the story on what she saw.

She told me how, when she opened the front door, the smell was horrible and there was peanut butter everywhere. "Why is there peanut butter everywhere?" she asked Kase.

"I gave it to my sister because she was hungry. I fed her peanut butter because she was crying," Kase replied.

Tracy told him what a good boy he was. When she got to me, she said I looked like a zombie, with my eyes dark and sunken in. It looked like my soul had left my body. She literally had to shake me out of it

PAINFUL GRATITUDE

to tell me to get it together! I told her I was so heartbroken and in so much pain, it was almost unbearable.

She said, "My sister, I have been where you are. It may hurt you, but this won't break you. Once you get over this hump, you will be okay. I promise you, you will get through this."

She went into the bathroom and ran water for a bath. She undressed me, walked me to the bathtub, and gave me a bath. While I was still a zombie, she washed me up and said, "You are strong enough. You are an excellent mom, and you are doing really well. You are young, but you have a job, an apartment, two beautiful children, and all your bills paid. You just don't give yourself enough credit. Thumbelina, you will get over this heartbreak, and years later you will look back and laugh at how silly all of this was."

She was right! A few days later I got out of the clouds and stayed busy raising my babies and started healing! If it wasn't for her, I don't know what would have happened to me or my children.

You see, Tracy knew who I was before I did. I clearly didn't know my worth. She had the ability to see who I would become and not who I was. That's why she was able to take a chance on me with her credit score. She saw my value and treated me like I was valuable even when I didn't know my worth.

When you know who you are, you will create a standard for yourself. You will make better decisions about the people you allow in your life and better relationship choices. Learn who you are and know your value.

Be Grateful

Whenever my children come to me with complaints, I stop them, put my hand up and tell them to say thank you. They can't stand when I do this because they feel like I don't care. Just because you have a complaint doesn't mean I want to hear it. The truth is, if you were grateful, it would change your perception of your issue or situation. Nine times out of ten, once you say thank you, you realize how small your problem really is and that you are complaining for no reason. There are people all over the world wishing they had your problems. Things could be so much worse than they are. Be grateful.

One of the most important keys to life is gratitude. Just knowing this truth has changed the trajectory of my life. To me, gratitude is a tool that changes our perception of a situation, softens the heart, brings comprehension and helps heal the pain.

Gratitude has played a major role in the past few years of my life. I would not be who I am today had I not gone through the things that I did.

After Dave's passing, I kept a gratitude journal. The following are some of the things that I am grateful for:

- I have had a child in my teens, twenties and thirties.
- I have experienced natural birth and cesarean birth.
- I have been single, married, divorced and widowed.
- I have been blessed to mother sons and a daughter.
- I have been able to travel in and out of the country several times.
- I have been blessed with a group of core friends who have been my friends for twenty years or more. Also, I am blessed with friends around the globe.
- I was a homeowner by the age of twenty-seven: a single, African-American woman with two children.
- All my husband, Dave's, hospital bills were set to zero through a gifting program from Memorial Sloan Kettering.
- I have worked for one of the most elite universities in the world in procurement with no real credentials.
- I purchased my mother's company and become a business owner overnight because of God's grace and my mother's obedience.
- I know who I am and the power I possess inside of me.
- I know my purpose, myself and my worth.
- I have learned to be the mother my children need and not the mother the world teaches we should be.
- All three of my children are healthy, smart and extremely kind, and all have a personal relationship with God.

As you are reading this, create a gratitude journal for yourself. Be present and quiet your mind. Write down all the things you are grateful for.

PAINFUL GRATITUDE

If you feel like you do not have anything to be grateful for, start with the things we all have taken for granted the most: our limbs (hands, feet, arms, legs, etc.). I promise it will change your life.

Go! Give it a shot. Say thank you. It doesn't matter how terrible life has been for you, say thank you. When you feel alone and hopeless, say thank you.

Be grateful.

Letter to God

11/12/2021

Dear God,

Today forty-three years ago, You sent me here to earth for a specific task.

It was probably the worst pain a spiritual being could ever experience because it meant I had to separate from You.

My love for You is so strong that I went willingly because I knew I would be coming back!

Not a day goes by that I wish I was home with You. In the meantime, I hope I make You proud. I hope You are pleased with my worship. I hope You are pleased with my lifestyle.

I hope and pray, when You do decide that it is time for me come back home and my work is completed, that I leave bits and pieces of You behind like You have told me to.

It is very painful here on earth because I know I'm probably the most misunderstood when it comes to You.

My love for You sent me here, and I know it's the same love that will send me back.

As painful as it is, thank You for choosing me to come here on Your behalf. My love promises to complete this journey in excellence. See You soon!

    Love,
        Your daughter